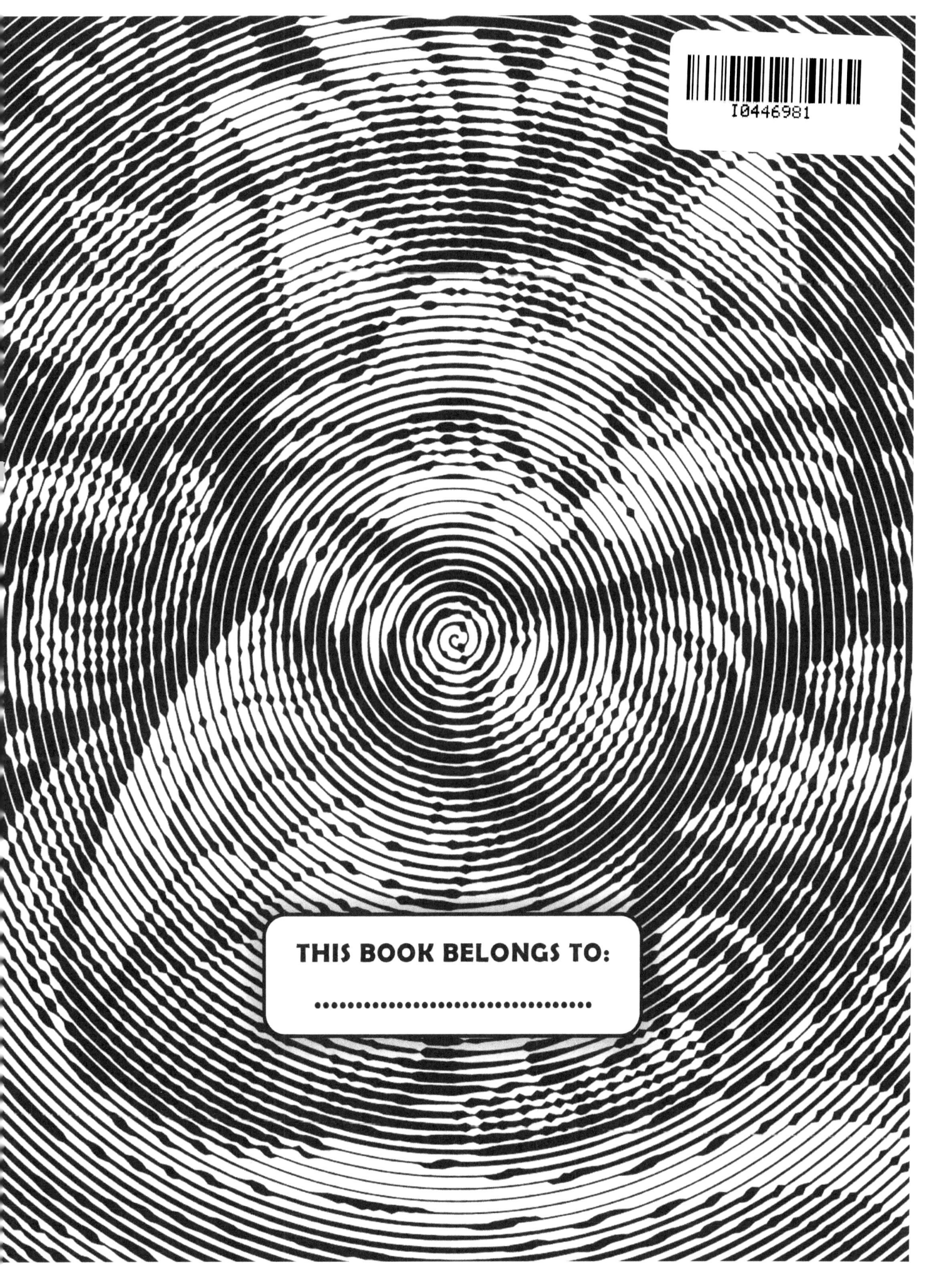

THIS BOOK BELONGS TO:

....

THANK YOU FOR CHOOSING US
TRY OUR OTHER COLORING BOOKS ON AMAZON
- Lily Ann Coloring Book -

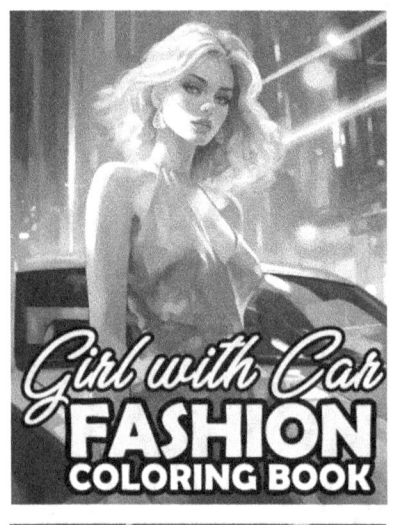
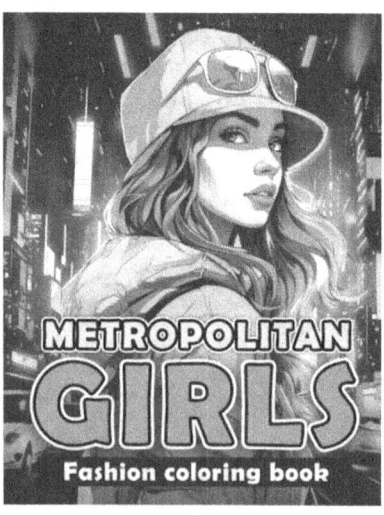
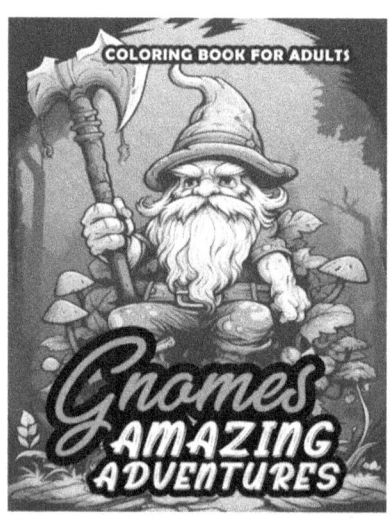
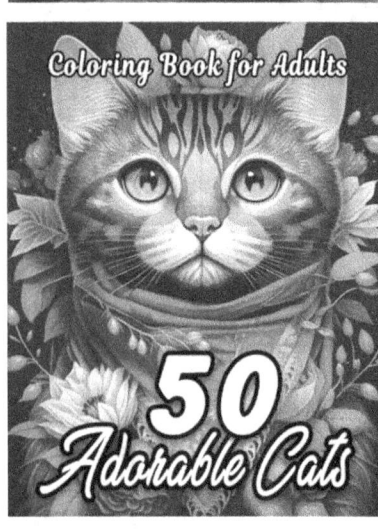
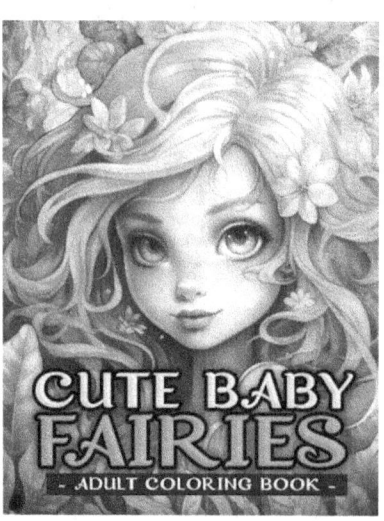
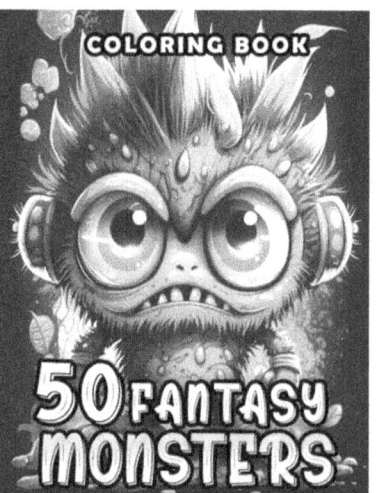
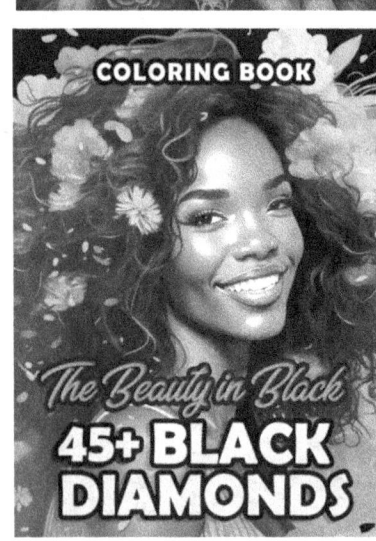
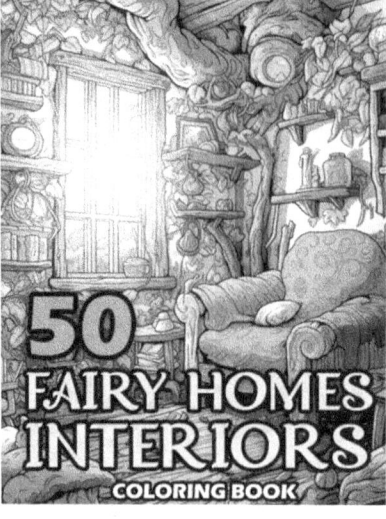
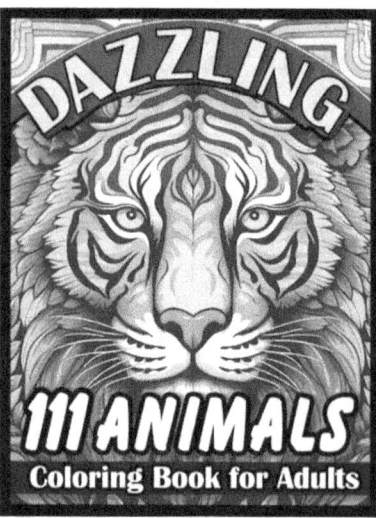

Thank you for choosing this coloring book!
Please consider leaving a positive review on
Amazon. It would mean a lot to me and help
other customers find the book.
Your feedback is greatly appreciated!

★★★★★

♡ **Get Free Printable Coloring Pages** ♡
& Join Our Community!

https://linktr.ee/5ideas.publishing

- Lily Ann Coloring Book -

THANK YOU!

Where to start coloring?

For the spiral coloring pages
Start coloring by filling the linesfrom inside as shown here

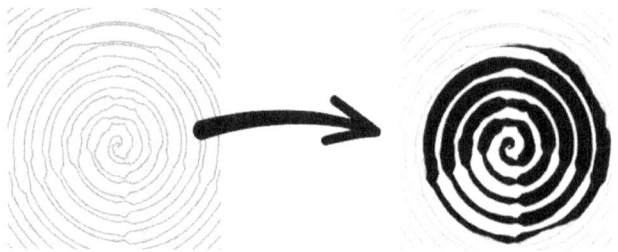

For the lines coloring pages:
Start coloring by filling the linesfrom upper lines
or the lower linesas shown here.

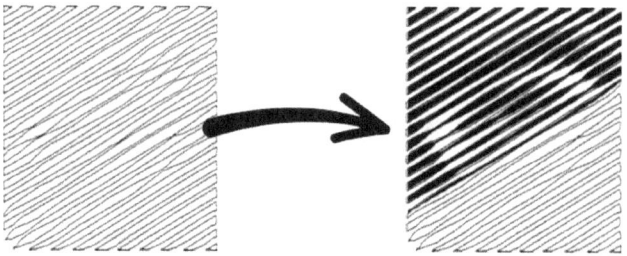

For the dots coloring pages:
Start coloring by filling inside the dots.

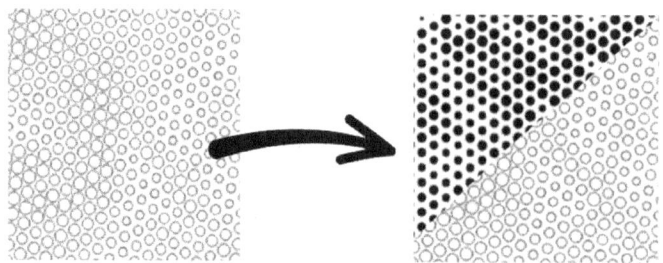

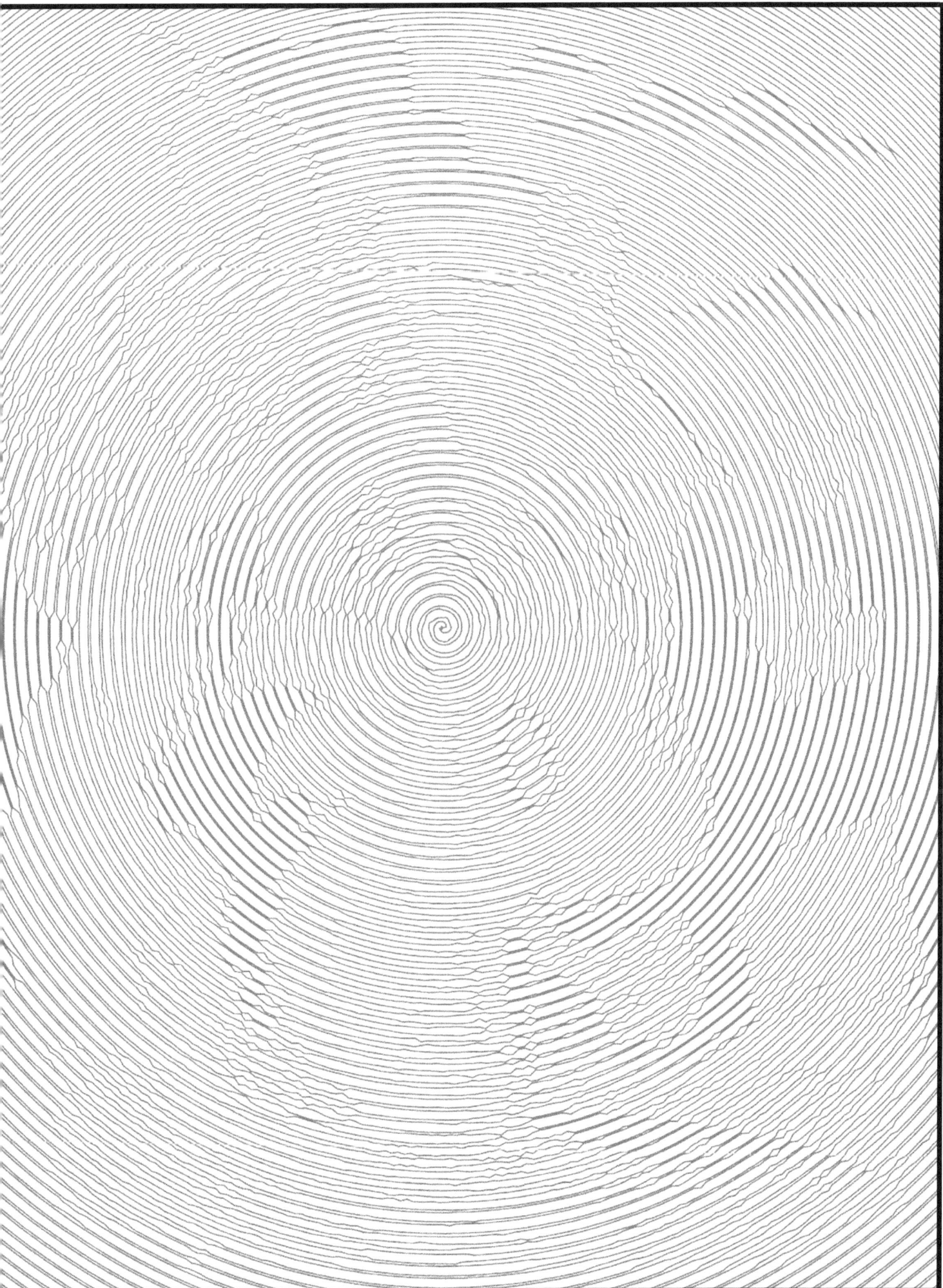

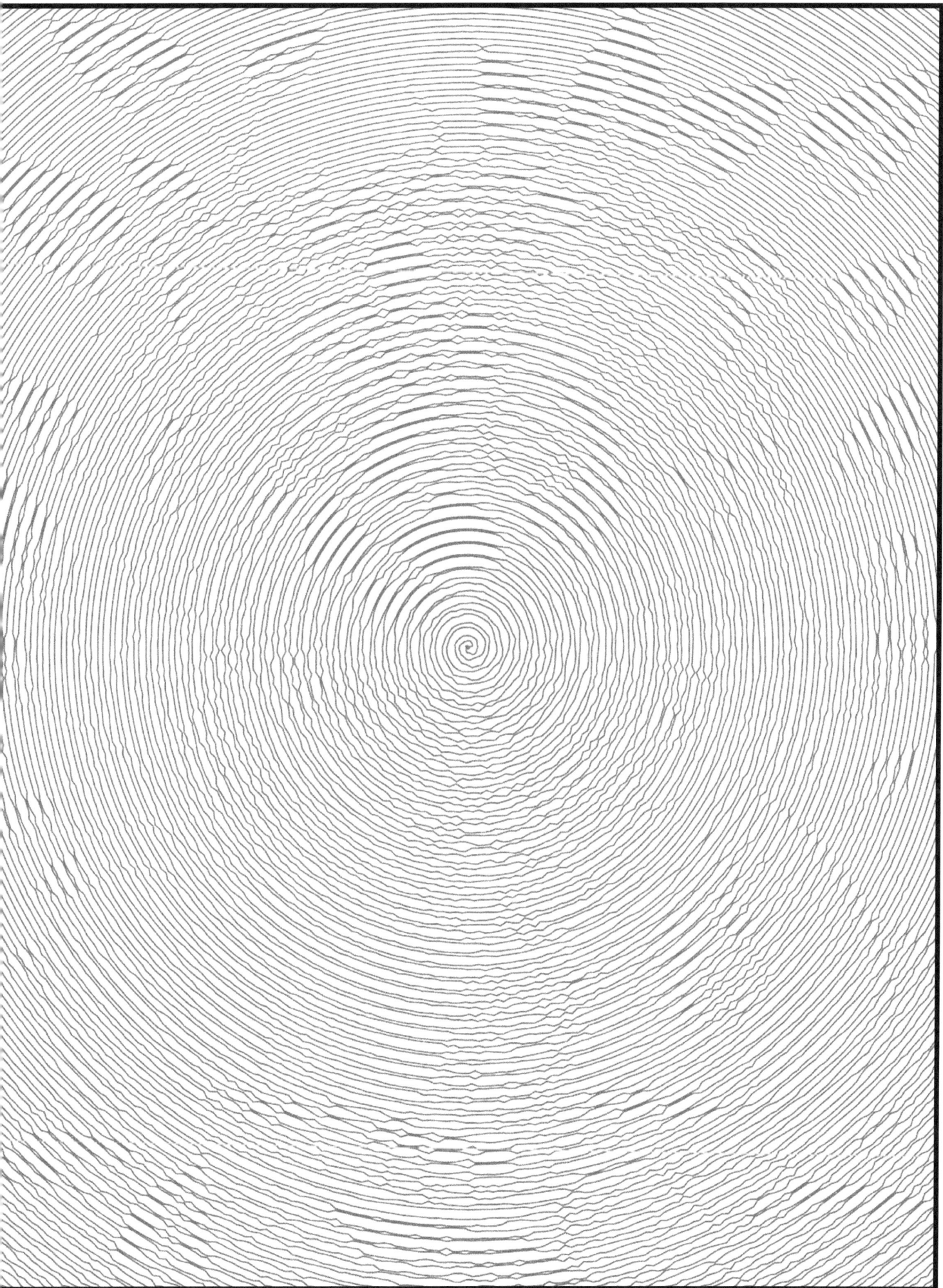

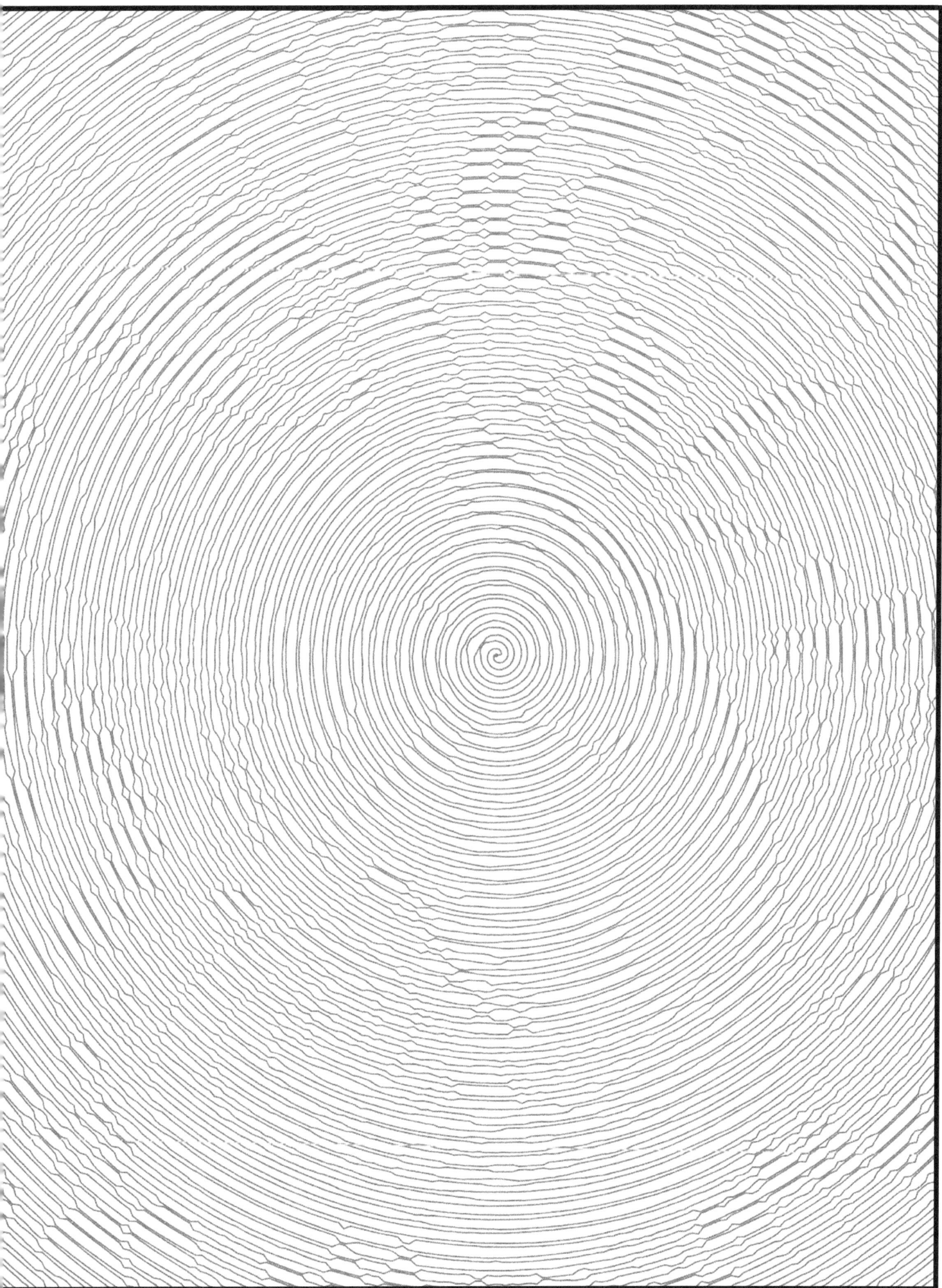

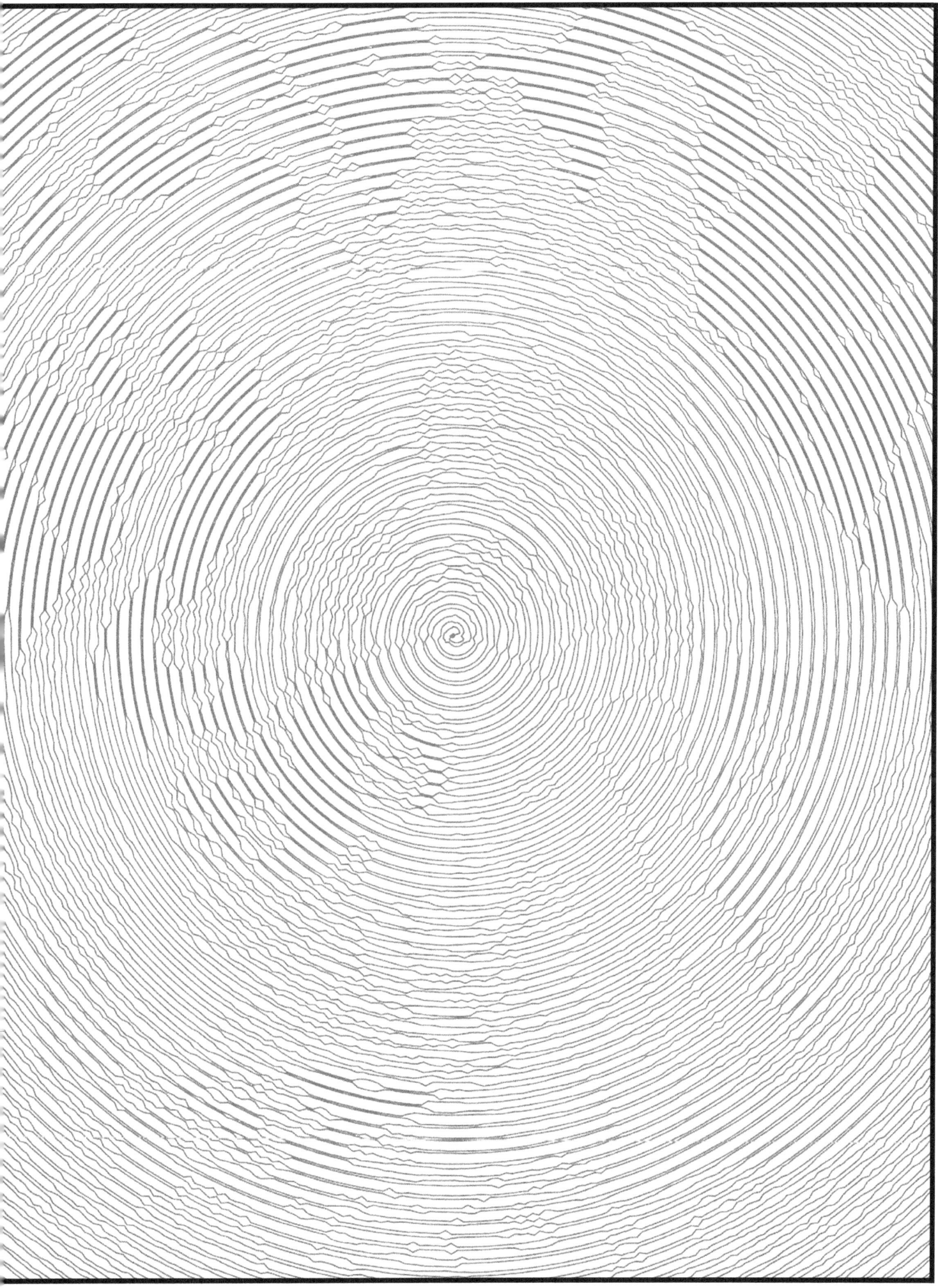

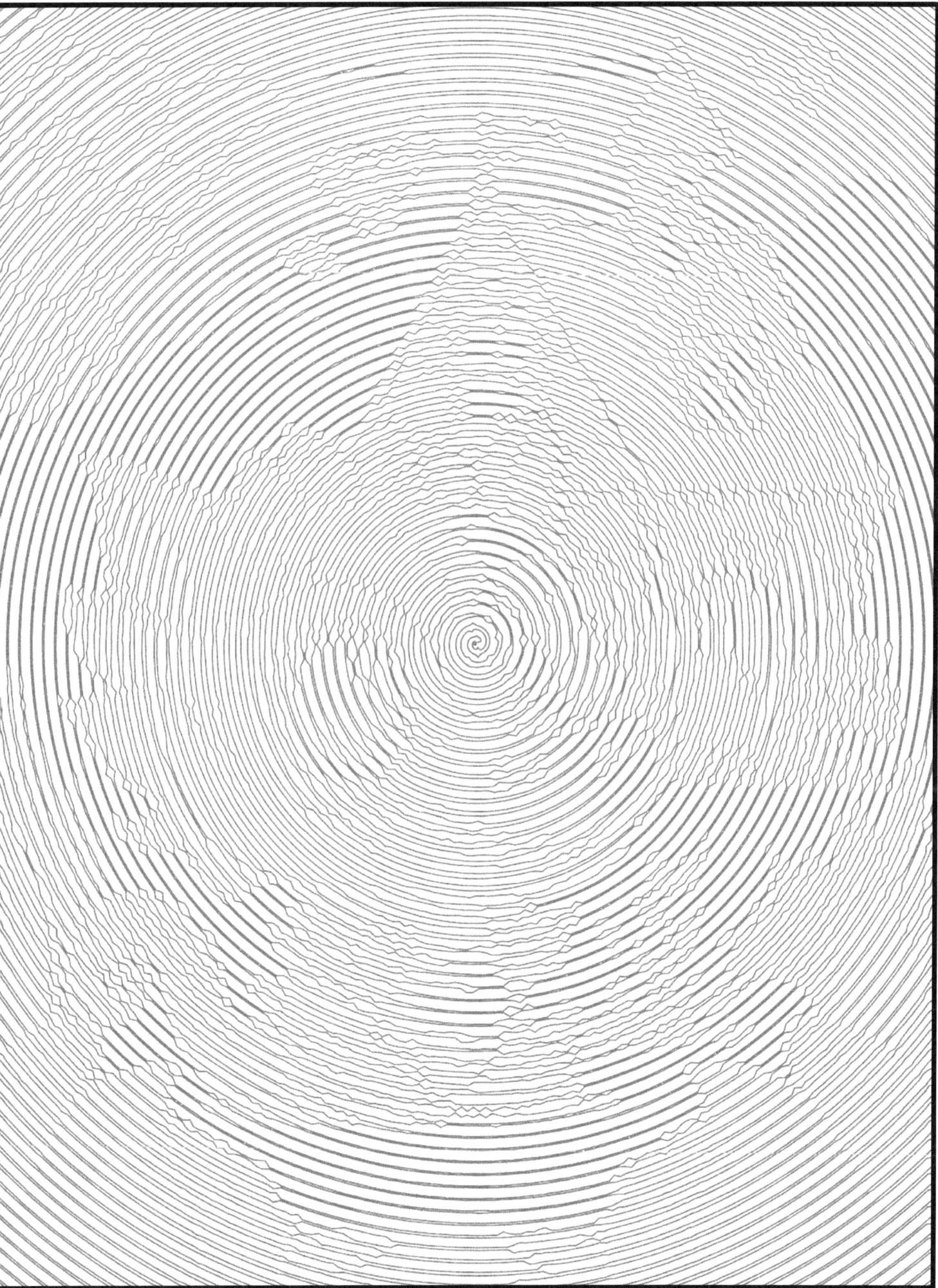

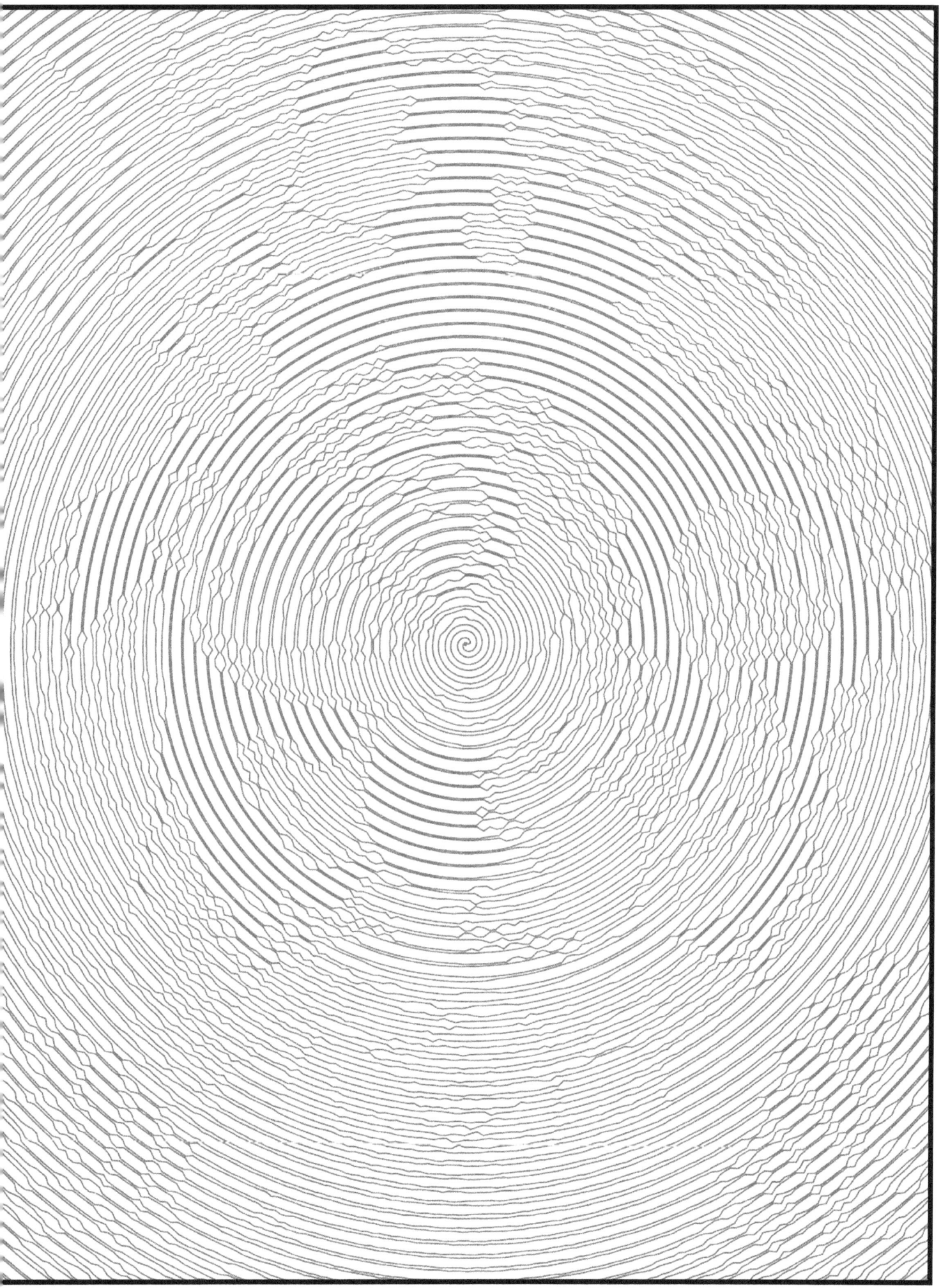

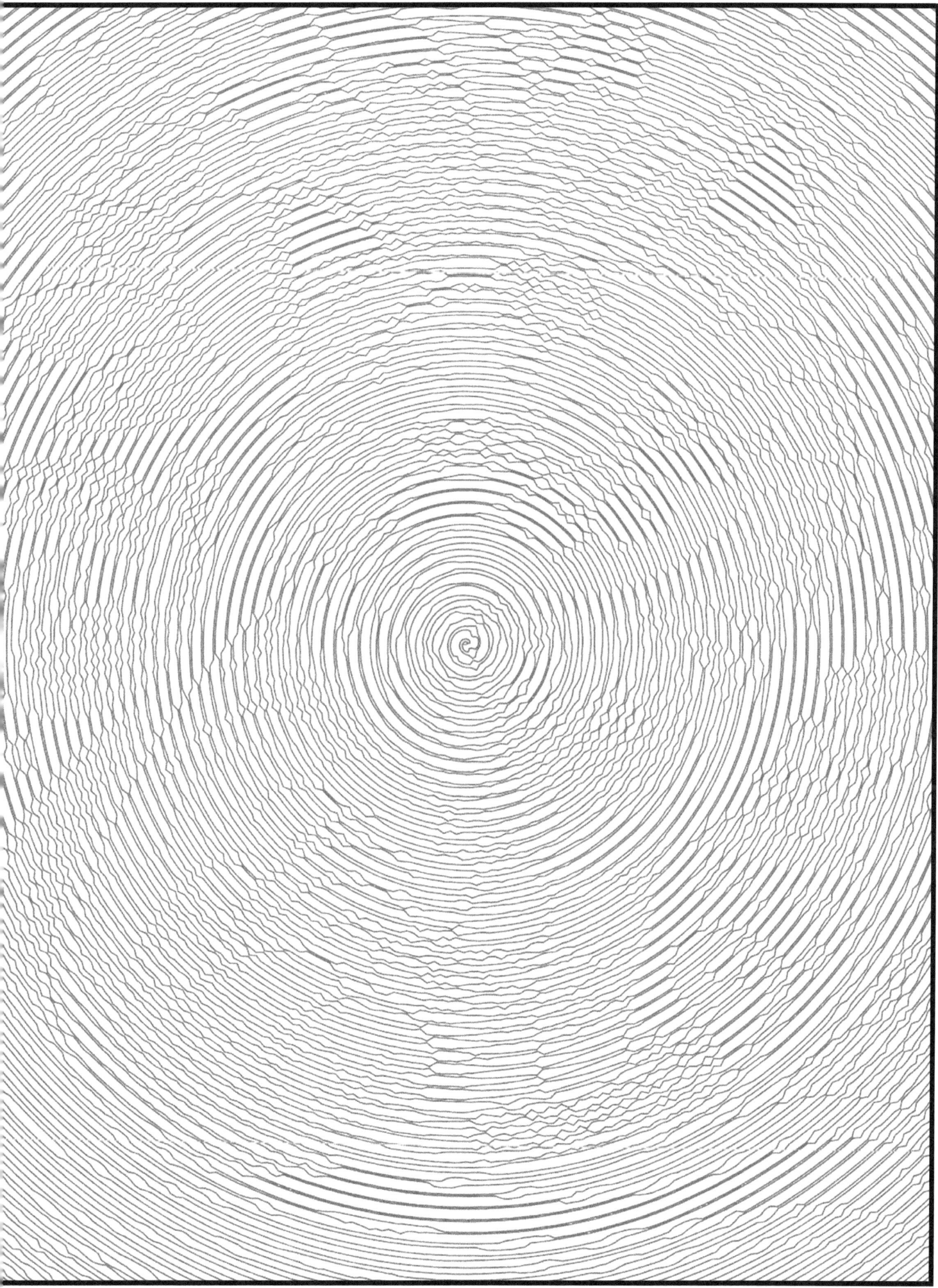

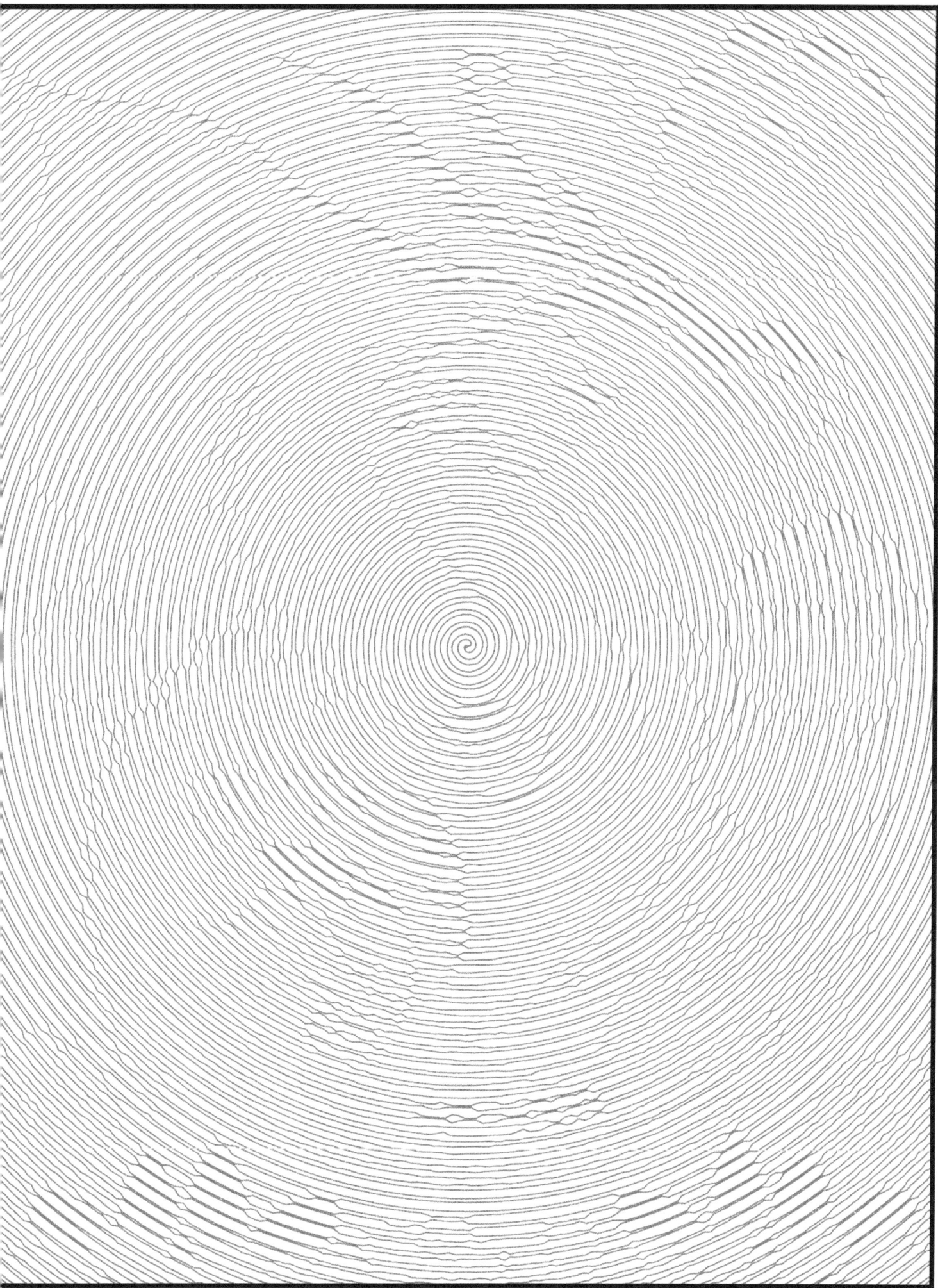

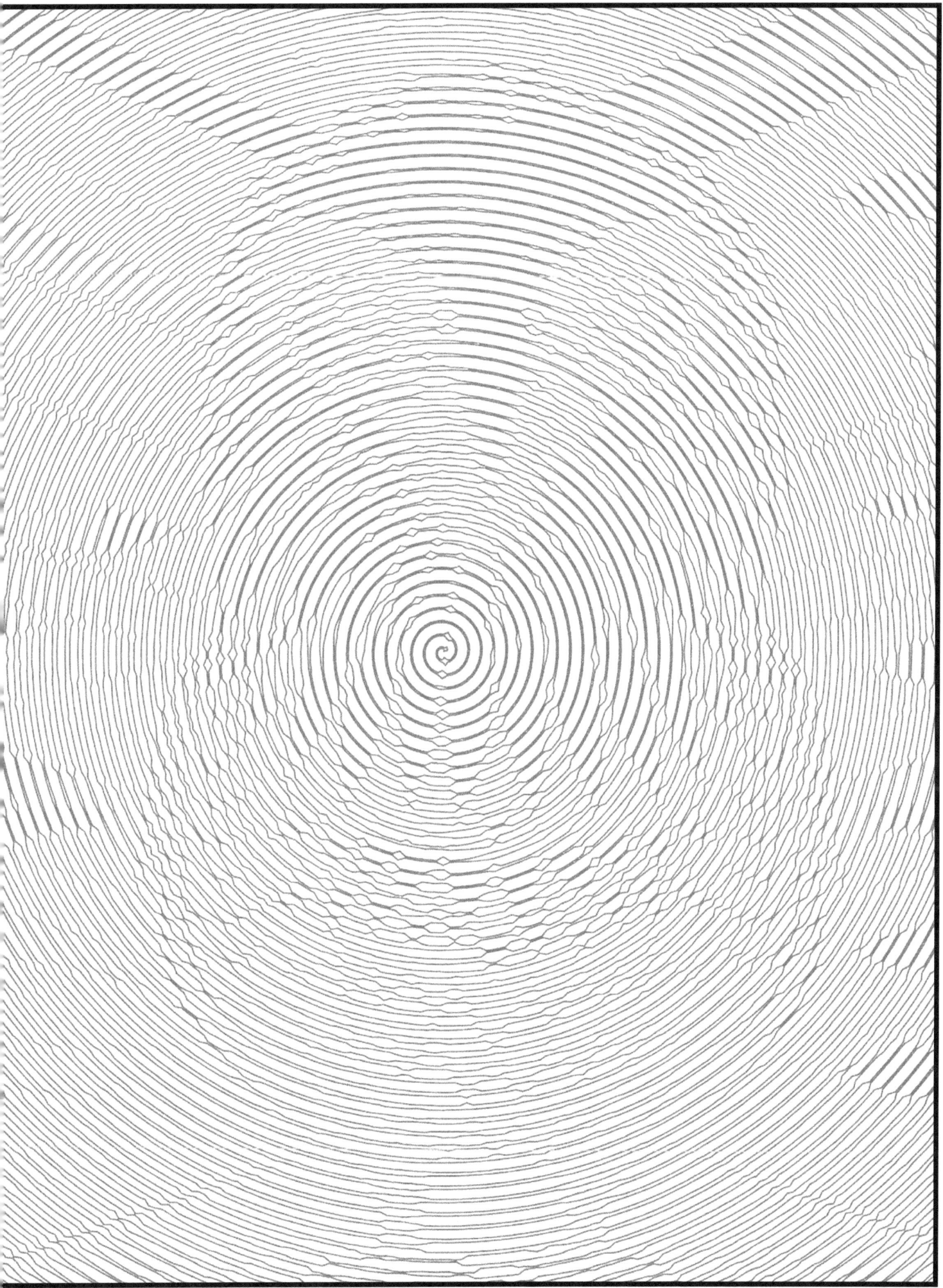

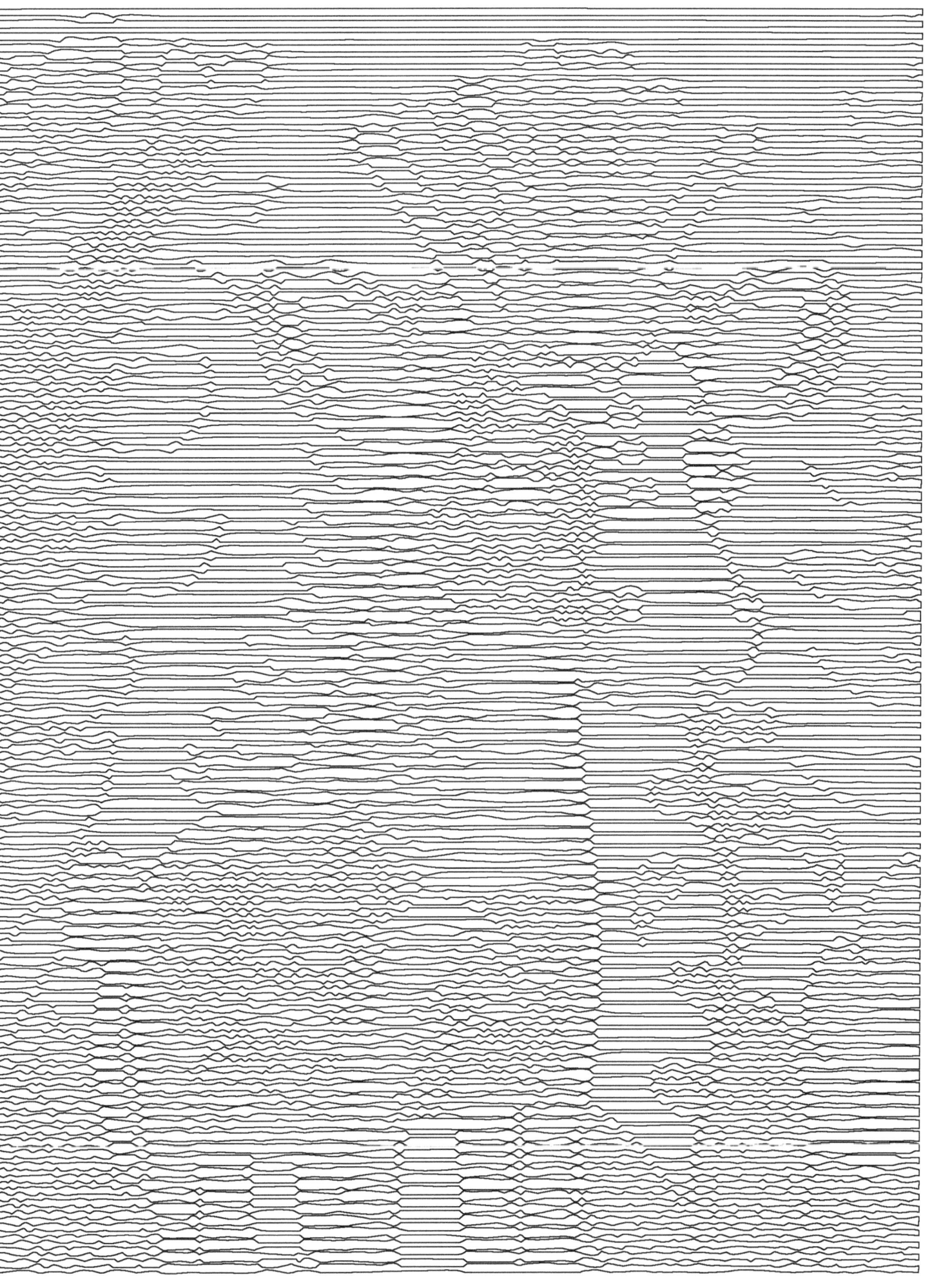

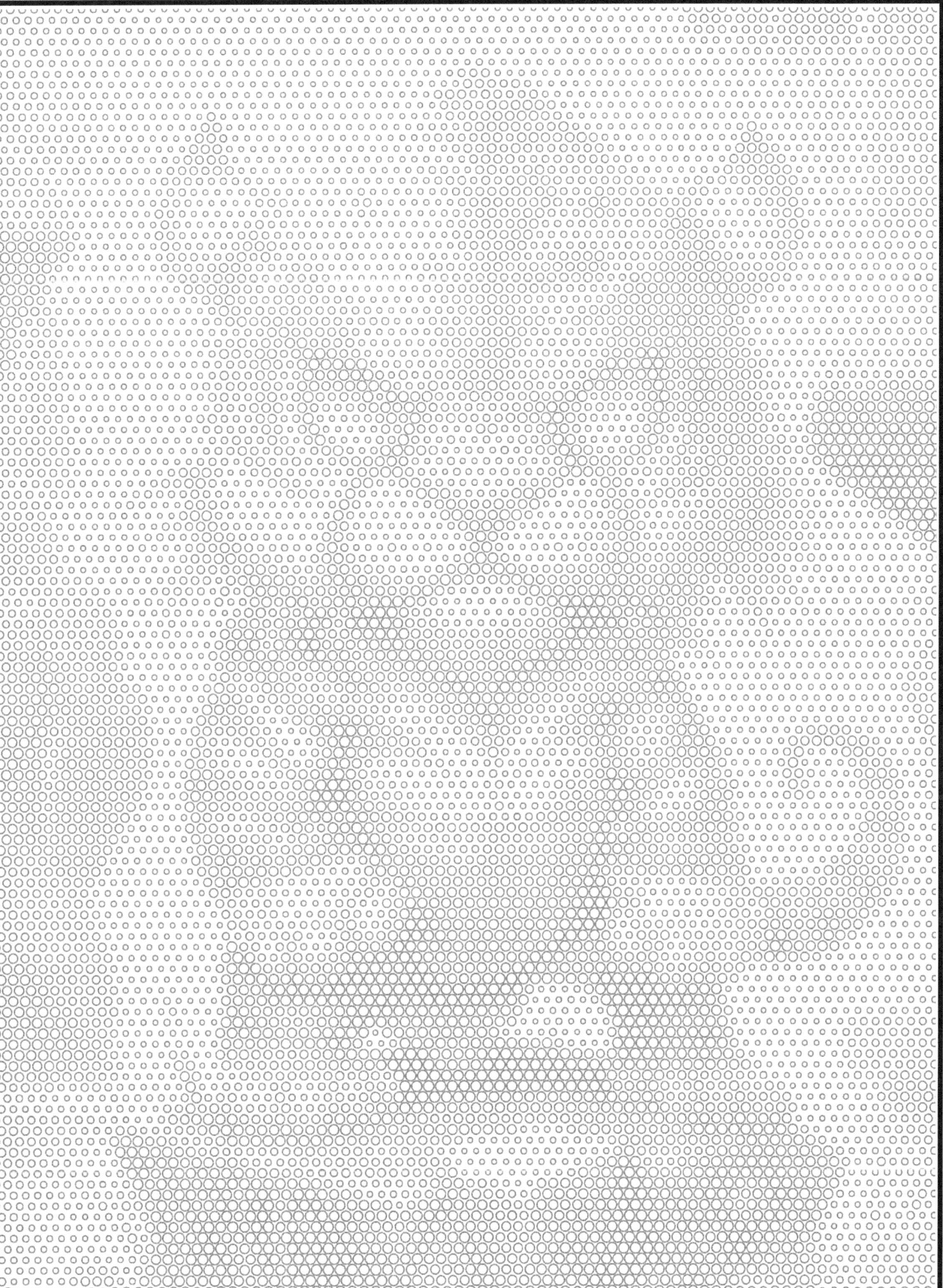

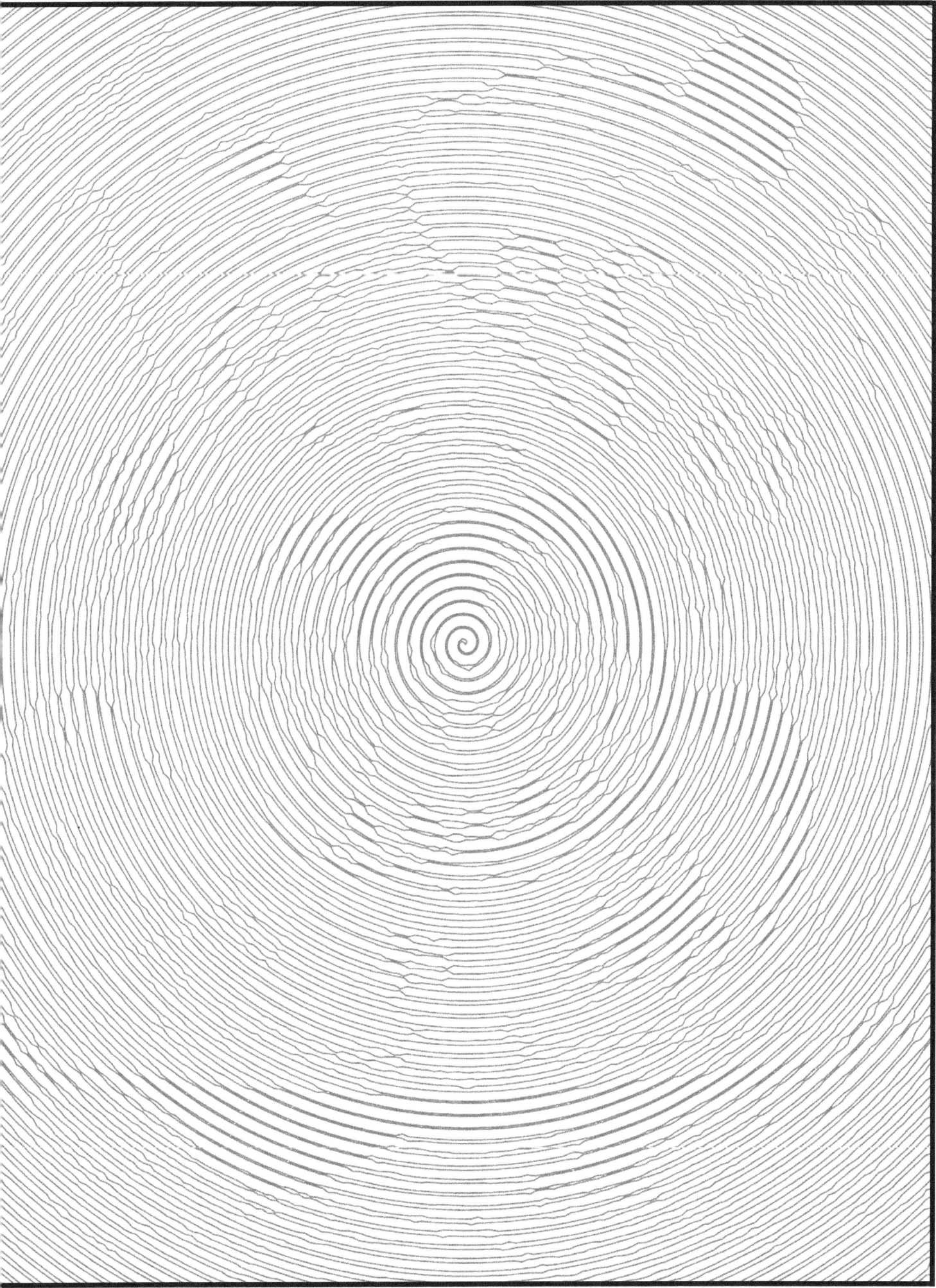

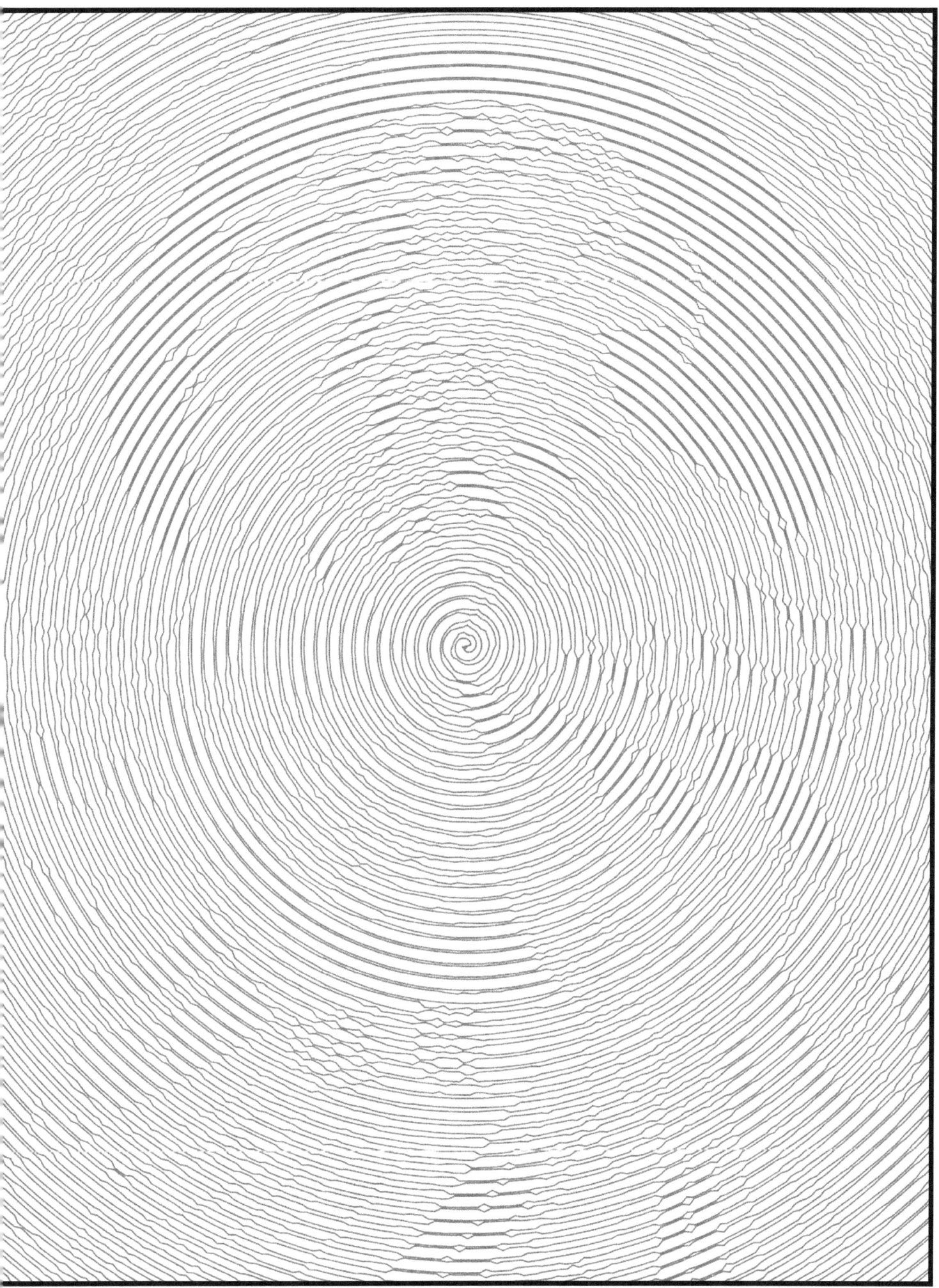

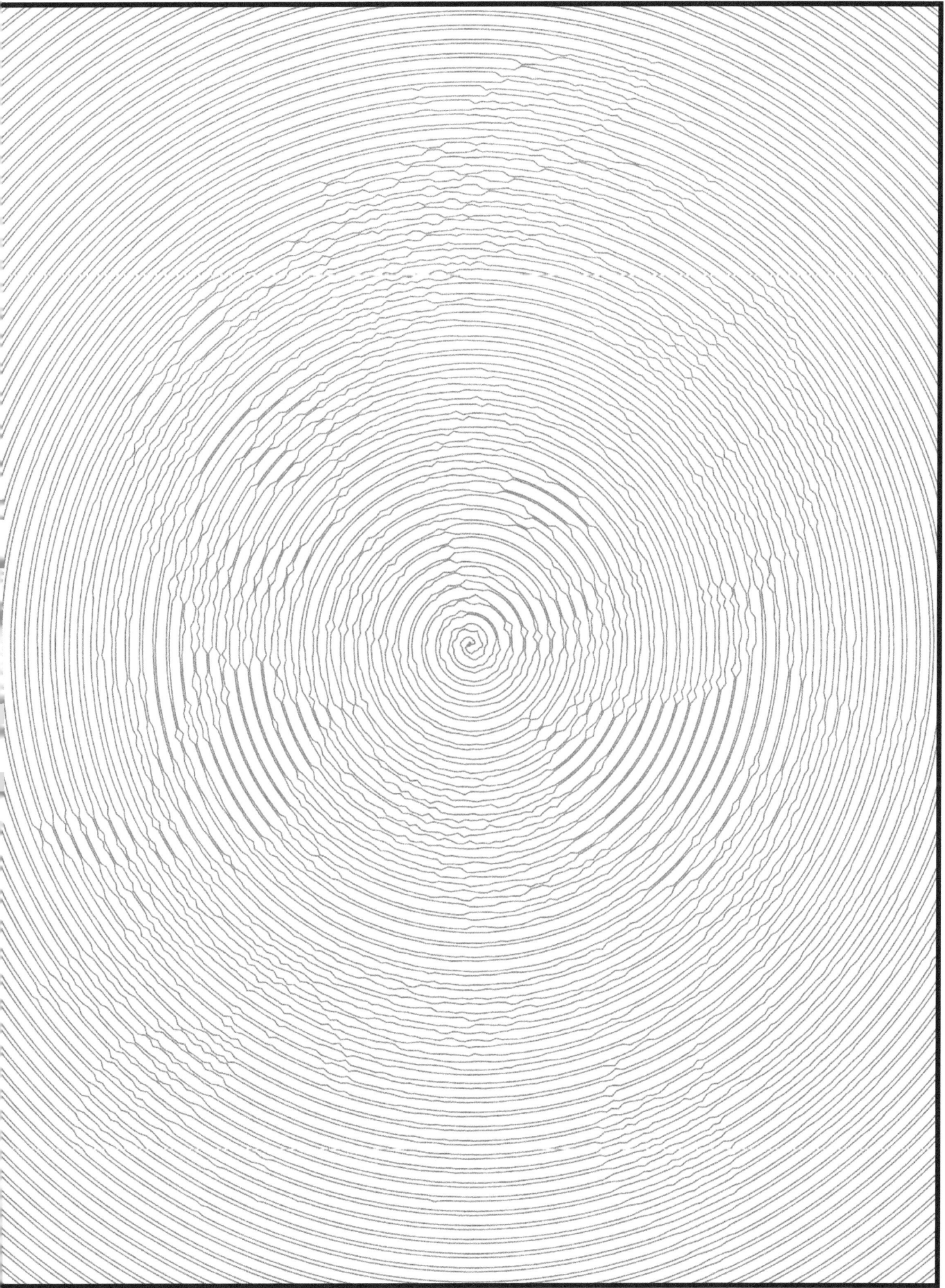

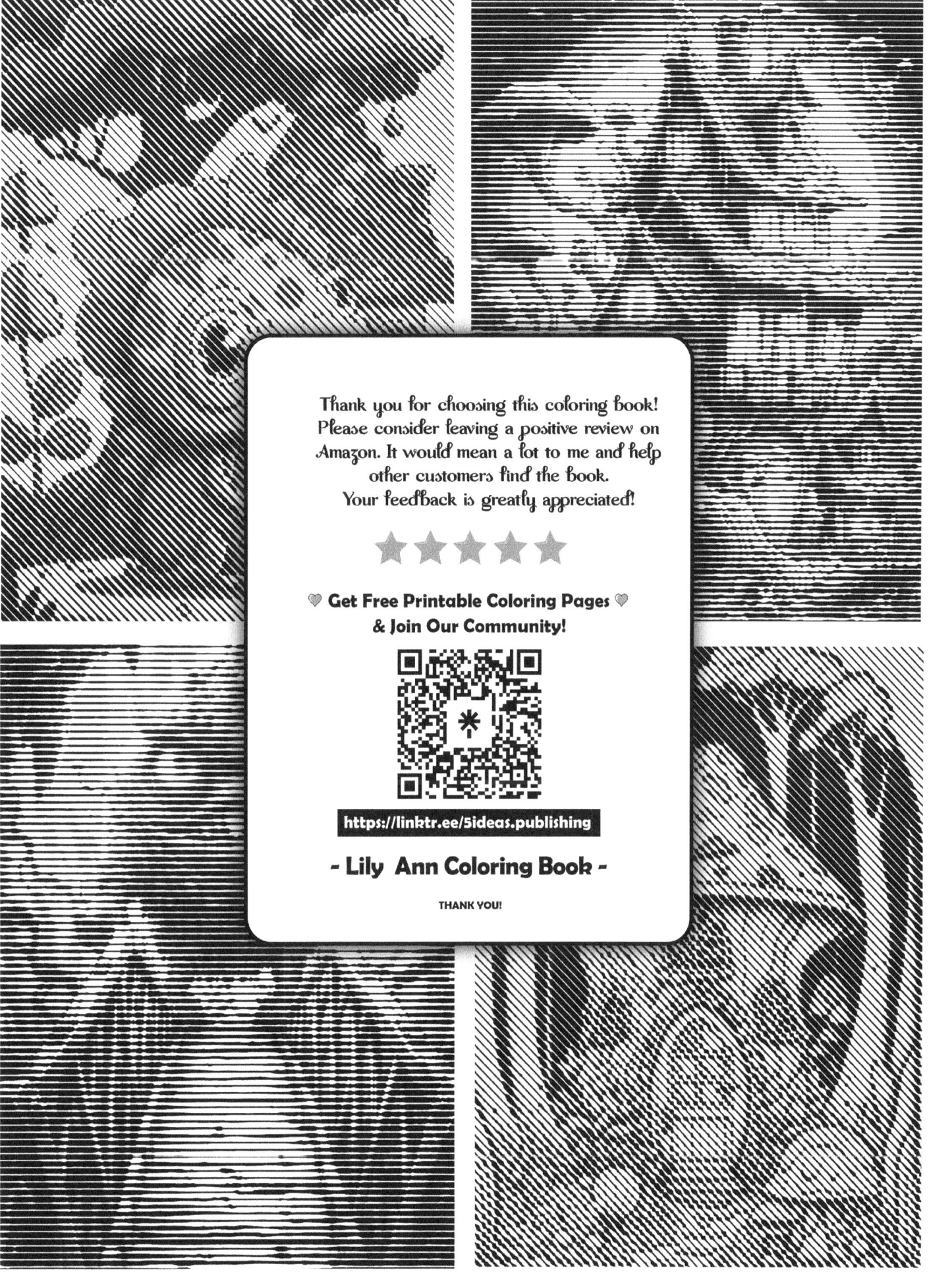

Thank you for choosing this coloring book!
Please consider leaving a positive review on
Amazon. It would mean a lot to me and help
other customers find the book.
Your feedback is greatly appreciated!

★★★★★

♡ Get Free Printable Coloring Pages ♡
& Join Our Community!

https://linktr.ee/5ideas.publishing

- Lily Ann Coloring Book -

THANK YOU!